Elephants

by Helen Orme

ticktock

Copyright © ticktock Entertainment Ltd 2006
First published in Great Britain in 2006 by ticktock Media Ltd.,
Unit 2, Orchard Business Centre, North Farm Road,
Tunbridge Wells, Kent, TN2 3XF
ISBN 1 84696 082 7 pbk
Printed in China

We would like to thank our consultants: The Born Free Foundation -
www.bornfree.org.uk

Picture credits
t=top, b=bottom, c=centre, l-left, r=right
Corbis: 16bl, 20-21, 22-23, 28t. Shutterstock: OFC, 1, 2, 4-5, 6-7, 8-9, 10-11, 12, 15, 18, 19, 25t, 25c,
26, 27, 28b, 29, 31, 32. Superstock: 11bl, 13, 14, 16-17, 24b.
Every effort has been made to trace the copyright holders, and we apologise in advance for any
unintentional omissions. We would be pleased to insert the appropriate acknowledgements in any
subsequent edition of this publication.

CONTENTS

Words that appear **in bold** are explained in the glossary.

THE BIGGEST OF THEM ALL

Elephants are the world's largest land-living mammals.

These clever animals can survive in many different **habitats**, from the open **savannahs** of Africa to the forests of Asia. Elephants can even survive in deserts.

Desert elephants in Namibia, Africa, may drink only once in three or four days. They are experts at searching for food over a wide area.

ELEPHANT FACT

There are two types of elephant, the African and the Asian.

This picture shows a young Asian elephant.

Elephants have no natural **predators** or enemies, but life is becoming difficult for them.

A family of African elephants.

AFRICAN ELEPHANTS

African elephants are the biggest type. They live in the central and southern part of Africa, on open plains and dry deserts. Some African elephants live in forests.

In some parts of Africa there are still lots of elephants. But even in these areas they are under threat from **poaching**, farming and **climate change**.

Both male and female African elephants have tusks. They use them for digging up roots to eat.

Bull, or male elephants, also use their huge tusks for fighting.

Two young bull elephants practise fighting with their small tusks.

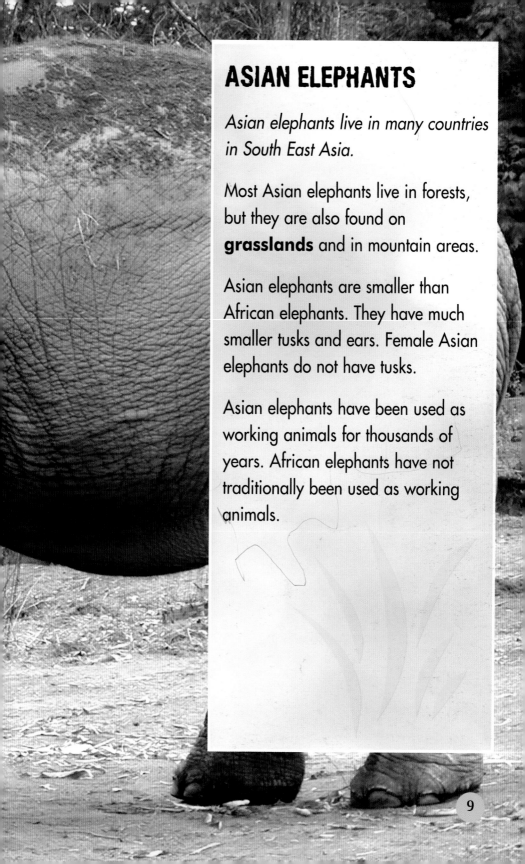

ASIAN ELEPHANTS

Asian elephants live in many countries in South East Asia.

Most Asian elephants live in forests, but they are also found on **grasslands** and in mountain areas.

Asian elephants are smaller than African elephants. They have much smaller tusks and ears. Female Asian elephants do not have tusks.

Asian elephants have been used as working animals for thousands of years. African elephants have not traditionally been used as working animals.

ELEPHANT LIFE

Females and young elephants live in family herds.

The herds often join with others to make large groups called **clans**.

Males leave their herd when they are about 13 years old. They live alone, or in **bachelor groups** with other males.

Female elephants are called cows. They start to have calves when they are between 10 and 13 years old.

All the cows in the herd help look after the babies.

ELEPHANT MUMS

Female elephants are pregnant for 22 months. This is the longest time of any mammal.

The calf in this picture has just been born!

FINDING FOOD

Elephants feed on different types of plants, including grass, leaves, branches, fruit, tree bark and even farm crops.

They eat a huge amount each day and need a big area to **forage** for food.

Each day an elephant needs to drink around 230 litres of water. Elephants are very clever at finding water. They can use their tusks to dig in the ground to find water.

Their digging makes waterholes that many other animals can use.

BABY FOOD

A baby elephant drinks its mother's milk. It uses its mouth to suckle, not its trunk. Babies start to eat solid food when they are about two years old.

AMAZING TRUNKS

An elephant's trunk is an overgrown nose and lip.

The 'fingers' (lumpy bits) at the end of the trunk can tell whether an object is big or small, hot or cold and what shape it has.

Trunks are very useful for lifting food into an elephant's mouth or for sucking up water. A young elephant must learn how to suck water up into its trunk and then pour it into its mouth.

Elephants often use their trunks like a shower to squirt water over their backs. Sometimes they blow dirt onto their backs for dust baths.

TUSKS

Tusks are very long teeth. If an elephant loses a tusk it will be difficult for it to dig for water or roots, an important food.

Baby elephants get their first real tusks when they are about two years old. Before that they grow tiny tusks about 5 centimetres long. These are called 'milk tusks'.

Tusks are made of **ivory**. This is worth a lot of money.

Hundreds of thousands of elephants have been killed so that their tusks can be stolen.

GIANT TUSK

The largest elephant tusk ever recorded was 3.5 metres long and weighed 97 kilograms – the weight of a large man!

A tame, working elephant gives rides to tourists in India.

18

WORKING ELEPHANTS

Elephants have been used as working animals for thousands of years. They are sometimes captured from the wild to be trained for this.

Asian elephants have been used to carry people and goods, lift heavy loads, pull carts and even carry soldiers into war.

Nowadays, many working elephants are no longer needed because their work is done by machines.

In some countries, looking after retired working elephants is a big problem. The elephants have to live in **sanctuaries** or **wildlife reserves** because they do not know how to look after themselves in the wild.

Some tame elephants have been trained to paint pictures! These are sold to raise money to look after retired working elephants.

KILLING ELEPHANTS FOR IVORY

African elephants have always been hunted for food and for their ivory tusks.

Ivory is easy to carve so it was used to make beautiful objects that were worth a lot of money.

It is now against the law to buy or sell new objects made from ivory.

Nowadays elephants are protected and should not be hunted for ivory. But poachers ignore the laws and still kill elephants for their tusks.

This picture shows tusks being burned. **Game wardens** have taken the tusks away from poachers. The wardens then burn the tusks so they cannot be sold.

A SAFE PLACE TO LIVE

There is another danger to elephants. They are losing their habitat as it becomes farmland.

Forest elephants are threatened by **logging**.

Wildlife reserves can help give elephants a safe place to live. But they need huge areas to roam in and lots of food.

If the reserves are too small, the elephants eat everything and there is not enough time for the plants to grow back.

WHERE DO ELEPHANTS LIVE?

Once, African Elephants lived across the whole of Africa.

Now they only live in the areas marked in red on the map. They live on savannahs and in forests.

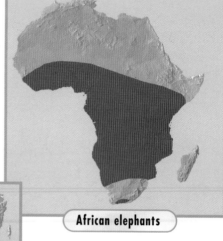

African elephants

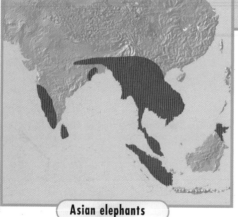

Asian elephants

Asian elephants live in forests and open grassy places in the parts of Asia marked in red. Some live in mountain regions.

• Because of climate change there have been **droughts** in many parts of Africa. Some areas where African elephants used to live have become deserts.

ELEPHANT BODIES

Elephants can live to be 65 to 70 years old.

African elephant

Weight: 4000 – 7000 kg
Height: 3 – 4 metres

Asian elephant

Weight: 3000 – 6000 kg
Height: 2 – 3.5 metres

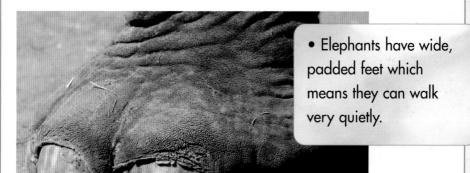

• Elephants have wide, padded feet which means they can walk very quietly.

• An elephant's trunk can grow to 2 metres long and weigh up to 140 kilograms. It has over 100,000 muscles, and no bones.

• Elephants can hold up to 6 litres of water in their trunk.

• Elephants can swim. If an elephant is in deep water, it can use its trunk to breathe – like a snorkel!

25

ELEPHANT FAMILIES

• The leader of each elephant family is called the matriarch. She is usually the largest, oldest and wisest cow in the group.

• Elephants will look after weak or injured members of their clan.

• Female elephants will have a calf about every four years.

• Calves weigh about 100 kilograms when they are born.

ELEPHANT FOOD

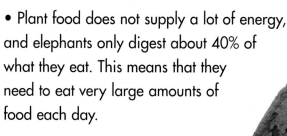

- African elephants eat mainly leaves and grass.

- Plant food does not supply a lot of energy, and elephants only digest about 40% of what they eat. This means that they need to eat very large amounts of food each day.

- Asian elephants will eat bananas, bamboo, berries, mangoes, coconuts, corn, jungle shrubs, palm fruits, sugar cane and wild rice.

- Elephants like salty-tasting things. They will look for salty-tasting rocks and lick these to get the salt they need.

ELEPHANTS IN DANGER

HOW MANY ELEPHANTS IN AFRICA?

YEAR	Number left
1979	1,300, 000
1989	600, 000
2002	400, 000
2010	?

• Some people think that it is a good idea to cut off an elephant's tusks so that poachers won't kill it. But elephants need their tusks for feeding. A third of the tusk is inside the elephant's head. This part cannot be taken away, so poachers will still kill the elephant.

• There are fewer than 50,000 Asian elephants left in the world.

• Asian elephants once lived across Asia, but as they were captured and hunted their numbers dropped.

CONSERVATION

• Wildlife reserves aren't always successful. It is expensive to put fences around a reserve. This means that elephants can wander from safe areas into unsafe areas. Poachers can also come in.

• Elephant numbers have gone up in some places. In others they have gone down. In some areas where numbers have gone up, there is not enough food for the elephants. This causes problems for other animals living in the same area.

• Many local people don't like the reserves. They think that the reserves take up land that they could use to grow food.

• One way to get people and elephants to live together is to involve local people in wildlife tourism. Many **tourists** want to see elephants living in the wild. These people need hotels and transport. They might also buy craft objects, such as jewellery and baskets, to take home. This means that there is work and money for local people.

Tourists on a safari holiday watch elephants from a Land Rover.

HOW YOU CAN HELP ELEPHANTS

• Find out about Elephants and other animals in danger. Do a project or a display at your school to tell other people about them. Find out about schemes that help retired working elephants in South East Asia.

• Join an organisation like the *World Wildlife Fund* or the *Born Free Foundation*. They need to raise money to pay for their **conservation** work. See the websites below for lots of fundraising ideas.

• Find out about schemes that let you adopt an elephant. (Don't worry – it won't have to live at your house!) See the *Adopt Wildlife* website below. You can also foster an orphaned baby elephant whose mother has been killed by poachers. See the *David Sheldrick Wildlife Trust* website below.

Visit these websites for more information and to find out how you can help to 'Save the elephants'.

The Born Free Foundation: www.bornfree.org.uk

The Adopt Wildlife website: www.adoptwildlife.org

The David Sheldrick Wildlife Trust
www.sheldrickwildlifetrust.org

World Wildlife Fund International: www.wwf.org.uk

GLOSSARY

bachelor groups Groups of young male elephants.

clans A family group of elephants. The clan will include mothers, their babies, young males and females and the matriarch (the female leader).

climate change When the weather in an area changes and stays changed. For example, an area which once had lots of rain may become very dry.

conservation Taking care of the natural world. Conservationists try to stop people hunting animals and they ask governments to pass laws to protect wild habitats.

droughts When there is no rain for a very long time.

forage To look for food.

game warden People whose job it is to look after wildlife reserves and the animals that live there.

grasslands Dry areas covered with grass where only a few bushes and trees grow.

habitats Places that suit particular animals or plants in the wild.

ivory The hard material that tusks are made from.

logging Cutting down trees for wood.

poaching The capturing or killing of animals by poachers so that they can be sold, or parts of their bodies sold.

predators Animals that live by killing and eating other animals.

sanctuaries Safe places for animals that could not survive in the wild. If possible, the animals live a semi-wild life.

savannahs Large, open areas of land in Africa where grasses and bushes grow.

tourists People who are on holiday.

wildlife reserves Places set aside for wild animals and plants to live. The animals and their habitat are protected by laws.

INDEX